THE PSYCHIC ARTS

ASTROLOGY

BY MEGAN ATWOOD

Consultant: Lisa Raggio-Kimmins, M.A., Psychology and Counseling

COMPASS POINT BOOKS
a capstone imprint

Compass Point Books, a Capstone imprint
Psychic Arts is published by Compass Point Books,
1710 Roe Crest Drive, North Mankato, Minnesota, 56003.
www.mycapstone.com

Library of Congress Cataloging-in-Publication Data
Names: Atwood, Megan, author.
Title: Astrology / by Megan Atwood.
Description: North Mankato, Minnesota : Compass Point Books, 2019. | Series:
The psychic arts | Includes bibliographical references and index.
Identifiers: LCCN 2018041937| ISBN 9780756561048 (hardcover) | ISBN
9781474769242 (pbk.) | ISBN 9780756561093 (ebook pdf)
Subjects: LCSH: Astrology—Juvenile literature.
Classification: LCC BF1708.1 .A885 2019 | DDC 133.5—dc23
LC record available at https://lccn.loc.gov/2018041937

Editorial Credits
Michelle Bisson, editor
Rachel Tesch, designer/illustrator
Svetlana Zhurkin, media researcher
Kathy McColley, production specialist

Photo Credits
Getty Images: Bettmann, 11 (top), Corbis/Found Image Holdings, 11 (bottom left); Newscom:
Everett Collection, 11 (bottom right), Heritage Images/Werner Forman Archive, 28, World History
Archive, 10; North Wind Picture Archives, 8; Shutterstock; Allexxandar, 4, CKP1001, 45 (right),
elwynn, 12, Everett Historical, 11 (middle), Oleksandra Mykhailutsa, 45 (left), Olena Yakobchuk,
cover, Photomaxx, 42, Rawpixel, 36, 39, Stepanek Photography, 44

Printed and bound in the United States of America
PA49

TABLE OF CONTENTS

CHAPTER 1

WRITTEN IN THE STARS: INTRODUCTION

Reach for the stars. Written in the stars. Wish upon a star. Thank your lucky stars. Any of these sound familiar? From these expressions alone, it's clear that people love to look to the sky for inspiration and answers—for themselves and others. And if you've picked up this book, you're right there with them! Maybe you've heard people around you say, "He's such a Leo," or "That's such a Scorpio thing to do," and you want to find out just what they mean. Or maybe you've been reading your Sagittarius horoscope for years and want to understand just why it seems to hit home. Is there more to this astrology thing? Can astrology help you live your life to the fullest? Can it give you some fun insight into understanding and helping others in your life? And what does it mean when Mercury is in retrograde, anyway?

This book will be a great starting point for your journey into astrology. Just remember: No matter what the stars say, no matter what your signs are, the ultimate author of your life is YOU. YOU get to make your own choices and ultimately decide who you want to be. But maybe, just maybe, astrology can help you on that journey.

GETTING YOUR ASTROLOGICAL BIRTH CHART DONE

Your sun sign—that is, your horoscope sign that is based on the month and day you were born—can tell you a lot about yourself and the people in your life. But to really dig deep, getting your birth chart done will take your understanding to the next level.

Unfortunately, doing your birth chart yourself would be way too complicated and would take years of studying. Luckily, there are many Internet sites that can help you out. A few things to keep in mind before you do it:

1. Get your parent or guardian's permission and help for this. This is not something you should do on your own.

2. Don't share any information online besides your birth information. Any site that requires your last name should not be used.

3. If the site asks for your first name, put in "Guest User." There's no reason for any site to even know your first name.

4. If a site asks you to pay for the chart, don't use it! There are many free sites online where you can get your chart done. Never give out any financial information.

5. Above all, if you or your parent or guardian feel uncomfortable with any site, don't use it.

Once you and your parent or guardian have decided to move forward, and you've found the site you want to use, you'll need your birth year, month, day, and time. Give as exact a time as you can; it should be on your birth certificate. Don't forget to include whether it's a.m. or p.m. You'll also need to know the city, state, and country where you were born. Once you've put in that information, you'll get your full chart or portrait with all your planets and signs.

In this book we'll be looking at the Western system of astrology. Western astrology uses the positions of planets on the date and time of your birth to create a natal chart—a chart that tells you aspects of your personality and tendencies. You could also do a chart right now of the planets and positions to find out the influences of the moment. The idea is that planets have a pull on all of us—and certain stars, positions, celestial bodies, and aspects influence events and personalities. You've probably seen your monthly horoscope in magazines, your daily horoscope online, and daily, weekly, monthly, and even yearly horoscopes in some of the same places. People seek out astrologers and astrological forecasts not just to help them understand what makes them uniquely themselves, but also to help forecast events and look into ways of living more peacefully with others. Astrology helps you understand yourself and others too!

NON-WESTERN TYPES OF ASTROLOGY

What we in the West know as astrology is not the only game in town, of course! Here are a couple of other systems:

INDIAN/VEDIC ASTROLOGY

Both Western and Vedic astrology use the 12 signs and constellations: Aries, Taurus, Gemini, Cancer, Leo, Virgo, Libra, Scorpio, Sagittarius, Capricorn, Aquarius, and Pisces. The difference is in the way each calculates the chart.

CHINESE ASTROLOGY, OR SHENG XIAO

In Chinese astrology, the year of your birth corresponds to a certain animal and the animal's traits. There are 12 animals altogether: Rat, Ox, Tiger, Rabbit, Dragon, Snake, Horse, Goat, Monkey, Rooster, Dog, Pig. The year starts on the Chinese New Year, and is a 12-year cycle.

CHAPTER 2

ASTROLOGY THROUGH THE AGES: THE HISTORY AND ART OF ASTROLOGY

Astrology is no passing fad. Cave paintings from 15,000 years ago have been discovered that have lunar calendars. These paintings also show constellations. Does that mean Cro-Magnon humans were astrologers? Maybe, maybe not. But what's clear is that the stars meant enough to them to paint them on stone!

Fast-forward a few thousand years, and there is evidence that the Sumerians noted how the stars and the constellations moved, which could point to early astrology—or, astronomy! Until the 1700s astrology and astronomy were treated as the same discipline. But it was around 2,000 years ago that the Chaldean people in the Mideast developed the wheel chart complete with zodiac signs and zodiac houses that we use to this day.

In the 4th century BC, King Alexander the Great conquered the Chaldeans and brought the knowledge of astrology back with him to Ancient Greece. There, the greatest minds of the day in that culture—including philosophers Aristotle and Plato and famous mathematician Ptolemy—embraced the system. The Romans adopted the astrological system from the Greeks, and the Roman names for the planets and systems are still used today.

The Middle Ages in the West were not easy for astrologers. The divinatory part of astrology came under fire from the Christian church, and from some in the Islamic world, as going against God. For centuries, ascribing meaning to the movement of the stars fell out of favor. By the 1700s, astrology and astronomy had become distinct disciplines. Astrology referred to giving meaning to the stars, while astronomy became the physics and patterns of what the stars were made of and how they moved. Astrology became popular again in the late 19th century. Mysticism started to gain a following in England, and the influential psychologist Carl Jung (1875–1961) used the system of astrology to point to archetypes that helped people understand their personalities better.

Carl Jung

The 20th century saw astrology become part of the mainstream. In 1908 an article in *The New York Times* mentioned that President Theodore Roosevelt would have been a different person if he hadn't been a Sagittarius. In other words, he would have made different decisions if he'd had a different astrological sun sign. The belief in this helped put astrology into the mainstream. Starting in the 1920s horoscopes were printed in newspapers and the astrological charts of famous people were published. Astrologer R.H. Naylor from Britain's *Sunday Express* paper began publishing astrological forecasts in 1930, adding to the popularity of astrology and even to a specific astrologer. After a prediction of his seemed to come true, the paper offered Naylor a regular column. Enthusiasm for daily horoscopes seemed to reach the stars. According to the American Federation of Astrologers, almost 25 percent of the United States population now read their horoscopes every day.

SO, PEOPLE READ THEIR HOROSCOPES EVERY DAY, BUT HAS ASTROLOGY EVER SHAPED WORLD EVENTS?

It sure did. Financial giant J.P. Morgan consulted famous astrologer Evangeline Adams for business advice. She found the dates that would be the best for him to invest in different businesses, and Morgan became a billionaire. He credited that to following her advice. In fact, it's rumored that Evangeline Adams told him not to get on the *Titanic*—a great prediction, clearly, if it's true!

Evangeline Adams

"Do NOT get on the Titanic!"

"OK. Fine."

J.P. Morgan

General Charles de Gaulle—a general who led the French in resisting Nazi Germany and who reestablished democracy in France after World War II—had a personal astrologer he consulted before making any major decisions.

Walt Disney is rumored to have used astrologers to make sure his opening events went well. President Ronald Reagan and first lady Nancy Reagan used astrologers and often changed plans or canceled events if the astrological timing wasn't right. Diana, Princess of Wales, used an astrologer to make sense of her tough marriage to Prince Charles, and any number of modern celebrities identify with their sun signs and talk about them publicly.

All this is to say: The sun is shining on astrology right now! And it's time for you to dig into your different signs and to listen to what the planets have to say.

DeWitt's *200 Year Calendar and Book of Horoscopes*, 1920s

Walt Disney

"It's opening day!"

CHAPTER 3

WHO ARE YOU? SUN SIGNS
AND THEIR ELEMENTS

At this point, you probably know what sun sign you are; that is, what sign you are according to your birthday and month. If not, read on in this chapter to find where your birthday falls.

There are 12 signs of the zodiac, and in Western astrology, they all fit into one of the four elements, considered to be the building blocks of the universe: Earth, Air, Fire, and Water. Each of these elements has certain characteristics.

EARTH:
SOLID, STABLE, GROUNDED, PRACTICAL

AIR:
QUICK-THINKING, INTELLECTUAL, COMMUNICATIVE, BROAD-MINDED

FIRE:
SPONTANEOUS, PASSIONATE, FIERY, ACTIVE

WATER:
DEEP, IMAGINATIVE, SENSITIVE, INTUITIVE

The words "cardinal," "fixed," and "mutable" are known as the qualities of the signs.

CARDINAL:
LEADERS AND INITIATORS

FIXED:
STABLE AND DEPENDABLE

MUTABLE:
SEEKING CHANGE AND UPENDING THE STATUS QUO

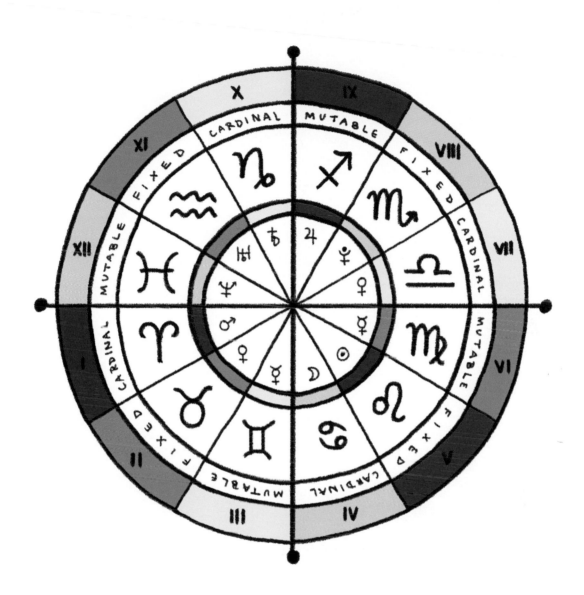

In the next few pages, you can see what your sun sign is and what characteristics describe you at your core. Even more, you can check your friends' and family's sun signs to get some insight into how they view the world. What a great way to understand the people you love even better!

ARIES

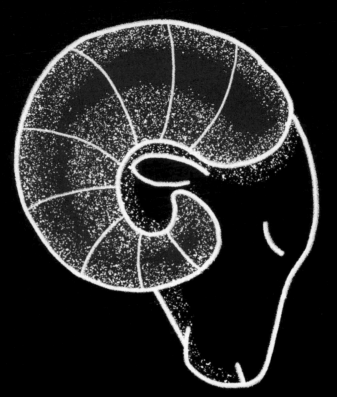

MARCH 20–APRIL 19

THE RAM

FIRE, CARDINAL

PLANETARY RULER: MARS

COLOR: RED

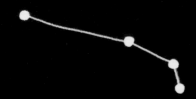

Aries is the initiator of the zodiac. You start everything off and love to lead others to success. As a cardinal sign that is also fire, you know what you want and you're not afraid to go for it. Have people called you headstrong? Willful? They're not wrong. But you are a great cheerleader for yourself and others and aren't afraid to push hard for what you want. You make a fiery friend, ready to take on the world!

TAURUS

APRIL 20–MAY 20

THE BULL

EARTH, FIXED

PLANETARY RULER: VENUS

COLORS: PALE BLUE & PINK

Slow and steady wins the race is your motto. As a Taurus you are determined, stubborn, and patient in reaching your goals. You're practical and grounded most of the time. Occasionally, you may BULLdoze over people if you think you're right. But you're still probably the friend people come to for advice! You weigh things seriously and make sure you think about your decisions. You're a hard worker and diligent in all you do.

GEMINI

MAY 21–JUNE 20
THE TWINS
AIR, MUTABLE
PLANETARY RULER: MERCURY
COLOR: YELLOW

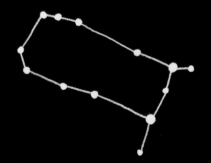

You are witty and fun to talk to—you almost always know what to say. You love to discuss everything under the sun and can do that with anyone. You're charming and fun to be around, but also have a deeper, quieter side you keep to yourself. When depressed, you can slide into being a little judgmental and gossipy. But when you're the best version of yourself, you are an adventurous, fun-loving friend who is a blast to have at a party!

CANCER

JUNE 21–JULY 22

THE CRAB

WATER, CARDINAL

CELESTIAL RULER: MOON

COLORS: WHITE & SILVER

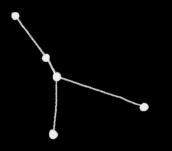

Home, sweet home is where you like to be. You love your friends and you love your family, and you prefer to hang out with them in your own home. Your sign is the crab—which means you may hold your emotions close to your chest. But wow, do you have emotions! You may have been accused of being moody, but people don't mind because you are loyal to the bone. You love to take care of the people close to you. Just make sure to make time for yourself!

LEO

JULY 23–AUGUST 22

THE LION

FIRE, FIXED

CELESTIAL RULER: SUN

COLORS: GOLD & ORANGE

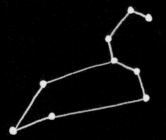

Leo the Lion loves drama, and you may fling yourself from one dramatic thing to another. You love compliments and need your adoring public to be vocal about, well, adoring you. But you're also loyal, kind, giving, and passionate! Plus, you are NEVER boring. You have confidence galore, and you're in love with life. You use your bravery and outspokenness for good and can be a natural leader and a loyal friend.

VIRGO

AUGUST 23–SEPTEMBER 22

THE VIRGIN

EARTH, MUTABLE

PLANETARY RULER: MERCURY

COLOR: BLUE

If you want something done right, ask a Virgo. You are great at the details, and nothing makes you happier than an organized space. You follow the rules. You know that the way to success is to do things by the letter! Has anyone called you a perfectionist? You may have the urge to redo things others haven't done to your standards. But you are kind and helpful, and you like using your considerable skills to help others.

LIBRA

SEPTEMBER 23–OCTOBER 22
THE SCALES OF JUSTICE
AIR, CARDINAL
PLANETARY RULER: VENUS
COLORS: LAVENDER & BLUE

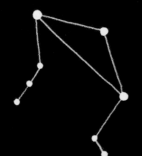

Do you have trouble making decisions? It's only because you can see all sides of an issue. Libras are all about harmony and beauty—beauty in the world and beauty in interpersonal relationships. You are charming and sincere, and you love love! Hopeless romantic? That's you. You're probably the style maven among your friends, and you do what you can to enhance harmony and keep the balance in any interaction.

SCORPIO

OCTOBER 23–NOVEMBER 21

THE SCORPION

WATER, FIXED

PLANETARY RULERS: MARS & PLUTO

COLOR: CRIMSON

Piercing, intense, magnetic, mysterious—you, Scorpio, are all that and more. You don't do anything halfway, and when you put your mind to it, world domination isn't off the table! You keep your cards close to your chest and take a while to trust people, but when you do, you will do anything for the people you love. You are protective of your people and are probably more than a little psychic. There is nothing shallow about a Scorpio.

SAGITTARIUS

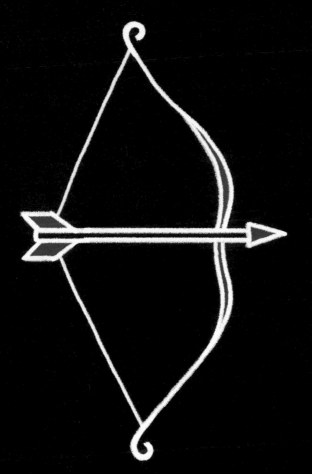

NOVEMBER 22–DECEMBER 21

THE ARCHER

FIRE, MUTABLE

PLANETARY RULER: JUPITER

COLOR: PURPLE

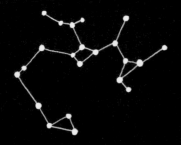

Camping? You say, yes, please! You are an adventurer, whether that is traveling the globe and collecting new experiences, or roughing it in the great outdoors. You do not like to sit still—probably more than one person has called you restless! But you're not all about movement; you also like to think about the bigger things in life. Whatever you do, you do with enthusiasm. You need lots of excitement and freedom to be happy. You love social events and developing your popularity, and you're great at both!

CAPRICORN

DECEMBER 22–JANUARY 19

THE GOAT

EARTH, CARDINAL

PLANETARY RULER: SATURN

COLORS: BROWN & DARK GREEN

You are practical and serious, but that doesn't mean you don't like to have fun! However, for you that fun must have a purpose. You have big ambitions—and the determination to make them happen. Your ideas are great. Even better, you have a solid, smart way of approaching the step-by-step process to make them happen. You are loyal and honest, and friends probably come to you to get no-frills advice that is ALWAYS helpful.

AQUARIUS

JANUARY 20–FEBRUARY 18
THE WATER BEARER
AIR, FIXED
PLANETARY RULER: URANUS
COLOR: ELECTRIC BLUE

Saving the world is your reason for being, Aquarius. But you're going to do it in your own unique way. You love getting behind a social cause and bringing people together. You are great at imagining what COULD be, and you're often many steps ahead of others. That can make you seem a little bit out there. But they just haven't caught up yet! You are visionary and philosophical and live to shape the world in new and exciting ways.

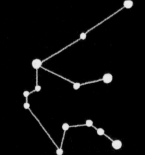

PISCES

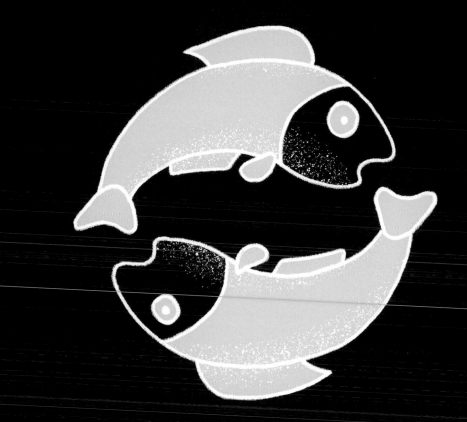

FEBRUARY 19–MARCH 20

THE FISH

WATER, MUTABLE

PLANETARY RULER: NEPTUNE

COLORS: TURQUOISE & PALE
GREEN

Boundaries are not really your thing. You feel all the feelings—even other people's! You're compassionate, empathetic, and sensitive, which makes you a caring and understanding friend—and also probably a little psychic. You also love to dive deep and talk about the meaning of life. You tend to meld with people you like. Though life can be hard because you are so sensitive, you are romantic and imaginative, and you make a great friend and partner.

CHAPTER 4

FINDING YOUR PEOPLE: COMPATIBILITIES

You know yourself a little better now . . . so how about yourself with other people? You may have noticed that you get along better with certain people than with others. If you pay attention to their sun signs, you might find out which signs mesh best with yours! Remember that your sun sign is only a part of what makes up your personality and tendencies—there are more planets and aspects in your birth chart. But a good place to start in determining who is most compatible with you is comparing the properties of your sun sign with those of other people you know.

Look at what element your sign is in. Very generally speaking, the following elements get along best together:

 **&** **AIR**

(ARIES, LEO, SAGITTARIUS)   (GEMINI, LIBRA, AQUARIUS)

 **EARTH & WATER**

(TAURUS, VIRGO, CAPRICORN)   (CANCER, SCORPIO, PISCES)

**Your element + someone else in your element:
Depending on how much you are like the other person
who has your same sign, you might be a great fit!**

Think about the properties of these elements. Fire needs air to keep burning, and water and earth mix well to make a whole new substance (mud). These elements are naturally compatible. An air sign with water, however, produces ripples on waves. Throwing earth on a fire puts it out. These signs are not QUITE as compatible. That doesn't mean it won't work out! It just means there are a few more obstacles.

Take a look at the next few pages to read which signs work best together. You could learn how to do that group project with people who seem totally different from you. Maybe you'll find out why you and your brother fight all the time. Or maybe you can reaffirm that you and your best friends were made for each other. This section could come in handy in so many situations!

 **ARIES**

As a fiery Aries, you like to lead things and to get things done. You're not one for games and you have no time for the wishy washy! The equally fiery **Leo** is a great match for you, as is the unconventional **Aquarius**. Shout out to **Gemini** and **Sagittarius**, though—these signs would also be good matches for your passionate self!

 **TAURUS**

A Taurus loves a stable, solid relationship and can be a fantastic anchor for the imaginative water signs. **Cancers** will appreciate your grounded approach to everything, and you will love their loyalty and emotional depth. **Virgo** also makes a good match—you'll be on the same page about how to approach almost anything. **Pisces** might be a little too imaginative for you, but the right **Scorpio** could be a perfect complement to your slow and steady pace.

 **GEMINI**

As someone who loves talking about big ideas and is curious about everyone, the inquisitive **Aquarius** is a great match for you. Aquarians' novel approach to the world and to big ideas will be a draw to you in a big way. **Libra**'s approach to beauty and the world will make you happy, and if you have trouble making decisions, leader **Aries** might just be a perfect person for you to hang out with. And for that restless spirit, grab a **Sagittarius** for some epic adventures!

 **CANCER**

It takes a lot to get close to you, Cancer, but once someone is in, they're in. The slow and steady **Taurus** is a great match for you and can keep you grounded, but the deep-diving **Scorpio** will meld with you in a way that other signs can't. Romantic **Pisces** could be a great friend or significant other for you. **Pisces** loves connecting to others and Cancers love to take care of the people they adore!

LEO

As a fun-loving Leo, being friends with an adventurer suits you perfectly—enter **Sagittarians** and their escapades and you will be one happy lion! You would also do well with an **Aries**, whose tendency to start things and to make things happen fits right into the drama you enjoy. **Libras** would also be a great match; their love of beauty and harmony lets your light shine its brightest.

 VIRGO

As a perfectionist, you, Virgo, need someone else who is just as grounded as you are. So you work best with fellow Earth signs **Taurus** and **Capricorn**. The Taurean's measured approach to life makes you feel like someone understands you, while the hardworking and ambitious **Capricorn** appeals to that part of you that likes to work hard and come through for people. A **Scorpio** match would work well too—as long as you are strong enough to handle the **Scorpio**'s occasional stinging words.

 **LIBRA**

If you are a Libra, you love harmony and beauty, and the witty, charming **Gemini** suits your needs perfectly. As a passionate believer in balance and fairness, you are also well suited to an **Aquarius**—your talks will be long and legendary as you work through all the world's problems. Magnetic **Leo** would also be a great match in friendship or dating. Your support and calm demeanor would balance **Leo**'s need to shine.

 **SCORPIO**

Scorpios are known for their magnetic and piercing eyes, and all your relationships mirror that intensity—both romantic and friendship. You will accept nothing less than complete honesty from the people closest to you, so only those signs who can dive deep with you are a good fit. **Cancer** can meet you where you are and provide an almost mystical connection. **Pisces** can also swim in the deep with you, but will have to be ready for your darker moods. **Taurus** may help you keep your feet on the ground and challenge you in just the right way!

SAGITTARIUS

You do not like to be pinned down, but you do love other people. You need a lot of space in both your friendships and your romantic relationships. The life-of-the-party **Leo** is a great fit for you—a perfect match of two fun and adventurous people. **Aries** would also be great, as they love to champion others and encourage taking risks. The quirky **Aquarius** would also delight you; their offbeat ideas and kindness are a great fit for you.

 # CAPRICORN

You are down-to-earth and not messing around. You have things to do and to do well! But you need the perfect people in your life to support your ambitions and keep you from working all the time. **Scorpio** might be a good fit for you because your drives will be similar; but for long-term steadiness and relaxation, a **Taurus** would be a good match. Similarly, watery **Cancer** can remind you to ease off the work and chill out for a while!

 # AQUARIUS

Being independent is crucial to you. That means your best friends and significant others have to be able to handle that need. **Sagittarians** are perfect for you because of their adventurous spirit and tendency to go off on their own for bits at a time. Harmonious **Libra** and philosophical **Gemini** will also give you your space. For those long, deep talks you like to have, Gemini is the better bet, but **Libra** will appreciate your quirkier ideas and habits.

 # PISCES

You are a sensitive soul who loves to meld with other people, so fellow water signs **Scorpio** and **Cancer** are perfect for you to swim to the depths and mine what's there. Both signs can be hard to read, but your spot-on intuition gives you deep connections. You may also benefit from the more grounded signs. A patient **Taurus** or an earnest **Virgo** might be a great anchor for you when your imagination trips into overtime.

WORKING WITH THE HARDER PARTS OF YOUR SIGN

(AND GETTING ALONG WITH OTHERS!)

Now that you know who you're compatible with, does that mean you should stay away from everyone else? Definitely not! Your friends will have a variety of signs and the people you date probably will too. But you may have to curb some tendencies or support people in different ways than you're used to. Here's a quick guide to what you can work on to be the best you and to get along with other signs:

Aries: Work on your patience. You want to get things done, but not everyone has your go-getter attitude.

Taurus: Work on your spontaneity. You like to take your time to make decisions but sometimes it's fun to just let go!

Gemini: Work on sticking to one course of action for a while. Your sign is the twins, which means you tend to work on two or more levels at a time. Your decisions might be baffling to others and you may seem insincere because of this.

Cancer: Work on sharing. When you get hurt, you tend to retreat into your shell and stay silent. Open up about your feelings, and it will make you closer to others!

Leo: Work on being a supporting character. You love the limelight, but sometimes it's nice to let others shine too.

Virgo: Work on letting things go. As a perfectionist, it's hard for you not to micromanage. Try to look at the big picture and support people on a larger scale.

Libra: Work on making decisions. Your sign is a scale. That means you weigh everything and sometimes can't move. Not everything needs a pros-and-cons list!

Scorpio: Work on easing up. You are intense, and you want everyone else to be on your same level. Remember that not everyone can sustain your passion.

Sagittarius: Work on thinking of others. As a free spirit, you love being able to take off whenever you want or to say whatever comes into your head. Just remember other people's feelings!

Capricorn: Work on not working so much. Your ambition is admirable, but sometimes you overdo it and forget to unwind. Let some fun in!

Aquarius: Work on not detaching. You love lofty ideas, but sometimes you forget to come down to earth and bond with the people who love you.

Pisces: Work on boundaries. You tend to take on the characteristics of the people you love, so just make sure to honor yourself and your personality too!

DAILY HOROSCOPE

CLICK

CLICK HERE FOR MORE INFORMATION

CHAPTER 5

DIGGING DEEPER:
PLANETS AND THEIR ASPECTS

As mentioned before, the sun signs are only part of your overall birth chart—astrology has a LOT more to offer. This chapter will touch on some of the other parts of your chart that have big meanings. Looking at the whole chart is beyond the scope of this book, but you can find out more once you understand the basics.

LOOKING AT THE CHART

If you had a chance to get your birth chart or astrological portrait done, you'll see a bunch of planets and something called the moon and rising signs on a wheel with pie wedges. You'll notice that the pie wedges are called houses and that there are many different lines connecting all your planets. Where and how your planets sit in your chart in respect to each other (called "aspects" and "transits") gives you a greater picture of what your strengths and challenges are. But the three biggest influences in your birth chart are your sun sign (birth sign), your rising sign (or ascendant), and your moon sign. Let's take a look at how these affect you. Once you understand that, if your friends and family are willing to share information on their sun, rising, and moon signs, you can find out even more about them.

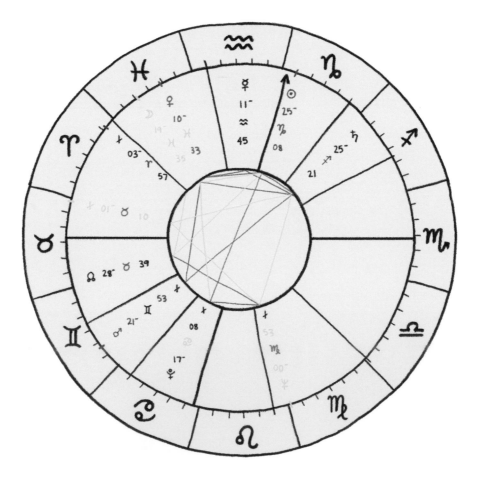

SAMPLE BIRTH CHART

RISING SIGN, OR, ASCENDANT

The ascendant is the sign that appeared to be rising on the eastern horizon the minute you were born. Your rising sign is how you appear to others. If the sun sign is who you are at your core—your immediate and intuitive reactions to things—your rising sign is how you move in the world and how you interact with others. So, if you are a Scorpio sun sign with a Leo rising sign, you might feel pretty intense and secretive about a lot of things. as a Scorpio would, but in public, you would love the limelight and seem carefree and larger than life. All these feelings are true to you—it's not as if you're making them up! But some of these aspects might just come out at different points depending on the situation.

MOON SIGN

The third sign in the triad of important signs is your moon sign. This is the zodiac sign the moon was in at the time of your birth. The moon is all about emotions and what your soul needs to feel whole. It also can play a part in how deeply you feel your sun sign tendencies. If you have a Pisces sun sign and a Capricorn moon, you might not be quite as sensitive and you could be a little more down-to-earth than if only your sun sign mattered.

The sun, the moon, and the rising sign make up the core traits and tendencies you see most often in yourself. But the following planets also influence you, so take a look at what else rounds you out!

HOUSES

If you were able to pull up or create your birth chart, you might notice that it is in the shape of a wheel, and the wheel is divided into 12 pielike shapes. These are called "houses," and the houses in which your planets and signs sit influence your personality and tendencies. On your chart, the houses are numbered near the center. Below are some keywords to show what each numbered house means:

1. Expression of self, public image, appearance

2. Money, possessions, what you value

3. Communication of all types, siblings

4. Parents, nurturing, home, roots

5. Romance, pleasure, drama

6. Work, day-to-day details, service, health

7. Marriage, deep relationships, companionship

8. Death, transformation, inheritance

9. Teaching and learning, travel, understanding

10. Authority, reputation, responsibility, career, public life

11. Hopes and dreams, philanthropy, social networks

12. Unconscious mind, secrets, karma, past lives

VENUS

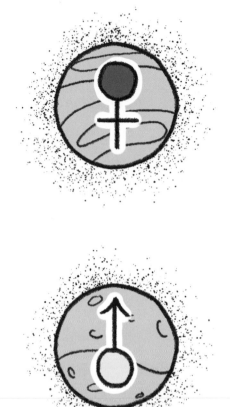

Where your Venus sits (which sign it is in) in your chart tells you how you like to be in relationships and how you feel about love. Or it can tell you how you feel about money, collecting things, and the finer things in life. This Venus sign can help you see how you relate to a romantic partner and what you need to feel good in a relationship. For example: If you have Venus in Aquarius, you need a lot of independence and space in your relationships, but if your Venus is in Cancer, you'll want to be close and deeply connected most of the time.

MARS

Your Mars sign shows how you like to fight. Mars is the planet of war and aggression, and whatever sign your Mars is in shows how you approach conflict and confrontation. If your Mars is in Libra, you will avoid conflict at all costs. If it's in Aries, you might relish an argument and the intensity it brings. Mars also shows how much ambition you might have or how much energy you bring to situations.

MERCURY

Finally, the sign your Mercury is in tells you how you communicate and think, and even how you make decisions. If your Mercury is in Gemini, you might be able to see all sides of an issue and occasionally have trouble making decisions. But you are a fantastic conversationalist, and you love thinking about big ideas. And if you're a Virgo, you'll need the details and the particulars of things before coming to a conclusion.

CHAPTER 6

MAKE IT YOUR OWN!

You can see that astrology has a LOT going on! There are so many different parts of your chart that contribute to who you are and how you move in the world.

The information in this book is a great start to help you find out more about yourself and your friends. You can also find out more about what's happening in the world according to astrology. For example, have you heard the phrase, "Mercury is in retrograde"? This refers to the different times during the year that Mercury appears to be moving backward in the sky (because of the way the Earth and Mercury are revolving around the sun). Since Mercury is the planet of communication, when it is "going backward," that means a lot of misunderstandings will happen, and tools of communication (think cell phones, computers, etc.) might not work well. Retrograde Mercury is a good time to revisit and finish old projects, but probably not to start new ones.

Pay attention to the movements of the planets astrologers talk about in horoscopes for the month and for the day. The more you steep yourself in astrology, the more you'll get a feel for what the planets do and what they mean. If you are really interested in digging deeper, you can read even more about making your own astrology chart and about the aspects and transits of the planets.

PARTY!

So you are armed with all this information about astrology and you want to share. It's time for a party! Some ideas for partying with the stars:

FOOD

You could make cookies or cupcakes and decorate each with a zodiac sign. Or you could make a cake and decorate the top with all twelve. Consider serving foods that showcase the elements, like these:

Fire: spicy cheese dip with hot peppers (make sure to warn people!)

Air: cotton candy that looks like clouds. Or you could provide foods from trees—lemon bars, apple pie, or seasoned almonds

Earth: french fries, carrot sticks, or other root vegetables. Or maybe put some gummy worms in a bowl.

Water: fish sticks, shrimp, or tuna salad and crackers.